Mary McLeod Bethune

A Great Teacher

Patricia and Fredrick McKissack

Illustrated by Ned O.

❖ *Great African Americans Series* ❖

ENSLOW PUBLISHERS, INC.

Bloy St. & Ramsey Ave.   P.O. Box 38
Box 777   Aldershot
Hillside, N.J. 07205   Hants GU12 6BP
U.S.A.   U.K.

To our friends Linda and Rob

Library of Congress Cataloging-in-Publication Data

McKissack, Pat , 1944-
    Mary McLeod Bethune: a great teacher / Patricia and Fredrick
McKissack : illustrated by Ned O.
        p. cm. —(Great African Americans series)
    Includes index.
    Summary: Traces the life and achievements of the black educator
who fought bigotry and racial injustice and sought equality for
blacks in the areas of education and political rights.
    ISBN 0-89490-304-7
    1. Bethune, Mary McLeod, 1875–1955—Juvenile literature. 2. Afro-
Americans—Biography—Juvenile literature. 3. Teachers—United
States—Biography—Juvenile literature. [1. Bethune, Mary McLeod,
1875–1955. 2. Teachers. 3. Afro-Americans—Biography.]
I. McKissack, Fredrick. II. Ostendorf, Edward, ill. III. Title.
IV. Series: McKissack, Pat , 1944– Great African Americans series.
E185.97.B34M37 1991
370'.92—dc20
[B]   91-8818
                                                             CIP
                                                              AC
Printed in the United States of America

10 9 8 7 6 5 4 3 2 1

Photo Credits: Library of Congress, pp. 4, 18, 23, 27, 29; Moorland-Spingarn
Research Center, Howard University, pp. 12, 17, 21, 24, 26, 28.

Illustration Credits: Ned O., pp. 6, 7, 8, 10, 14, 15, 16, 22.

Cover Illustration: Ned O.

Contents

Mary Jane McLeod Bethune
Born: July 10, 1875, Mayesville, South Carolina.
Died: May 18, 1955, Daytona Beach, Florida.

1

I Will Read!

It was the summer of 1875. Patsy and Sam McLeod's (sounds like Mac-Loud) fifteenth child was born. Her name was Mary Jane McLeod.

It was a happy time for the family. Patsy and Sam had been **slaves**.* Mary Jane was their first child born free! That made Mary Jane McLeod special.

---

* Words in **bold type** are explained in *Words to Know* on page 31.

Mary Jane grew up in a large and loving family in Mayesville, South Carolina. She rode Old Bush, the family mule, to the fields. She picked cotton along with her brothers and sisters on her father's farm.

One day Mary Jane went with her mother to a large house. Her mother washed and ironed for the people who lived there. Mary Jane had never been in such a big house. A young girl who lived there showed Mary around.

There was a book on a table. Mary opened it. Suddenly the girl took it away, saying, "Put that book down! You can't read it anyway!"

Mary Jane was surprised and hurt. True, she couldn't read. But why did picking up a book make the other girl so angry?

The McLeods had a Bible. Nobody could read it. That night, Mary Jane held the book in her hand. "I will read!" she said. "God willing, I will read!"

2

School Days

One day Miss Emma Wilson came to Mayesville. She told Sam and Patsy about the school she was starting. Would they send Mary Jane to school?

Sam didn't think so. He needed everybody to help in the fields. Mary Jane prayed softly. Patsy spoke to Sam alone. At last Sam gave in. Mary could go to school.

Mary Jane's brothers and sisters were disappointed. Why couldn't she read after the first day in school? It took time. Before long Mary Jane did learn how to read and write. On one special night, she read the Bible to her mother and father. They were proud.

Miss Wilson's school went to the sixth grade. A kind woman paid for Mary to go to the **Scotia Seminary** in Concord, North

Carolina. In 1887 Mary went away to school.

She was just twelve years old. It was so lonely at first. She missed her family very much. Seven years later Mary finished Scotia. Then she went to **Moody Bible College** in Chicago. Mary Jane McLeod was ready to start her life's work. But what would it be? she wondered.

3
A Dream and $1.50

Mary wanted to teach in Africa. Instead she took a teaching job in Georgia. Good teachers were needed there.

Mary met Albertus Bethune. He was a teacher too. He made her laugh. They were happy together. In 1898 Mary and Albertus married. A year later, their son was born. His name was Albert McLeod Bethune. Everyone called him Bert.

Mrs. Bethune heard there was no school

Mary's marriage to Albertus didn't last long. Mary moved to
Daytona Beach, Florida with little Bert. Albertus followed
later. He was not interested in starting a school. Albertus and
Mary lived apart.

for black children in Daytona Beach, Florida. Mrs. Bethune went there.

"I want to start a school for Negro girls," she said. All she had was $1.50. Some people laughed. Others helped.

Mrs. Bethune would not give up her dream. First she rented a small house. She found writing paper in the trash. She used

boxes for desks and coal for pencils. It was a poor beginning.

But, on October 3, 1904, Mrs. Bethune opened her school. She had five students. By 1905 the school had 100 students and three teachers.

Next, she bought land that had been the

city trash dump. That is where she would build her school. Some people laughed. But others helped. Rich, important people gave money to help build her school . . . and a hospital.

The first building was finished in 1906. It was called Faith Hall, because faith had built it.

Mrs. Bethune could pick up the telephone and call very important people and ask for their help. Some of the people who helped were John D. Rockefeller, James Gamble (of Proctor & Gamble), and Thomas H. White, president of White Sewing Machine Company.

Mrs. Bethune's school grew and grew. Here she is standing in front of White Hall with students. She also built McLeod Hospital on campus.

4

The Black Rose

In 1925 Mrs. Bethune's school joined with Cookman, an all-boys school. Bethune-Cookman became a grade school, high school, and college. Boys and girls went to school together.

Mrs. Bethune was the school's first **president**. But, to her students, she was always just "Mother Dear."

Another name for Mrs. Bethune was "The Black Rose." This is how she got that name.

Mrs. Bethune spoke all over the country. One idea she talked about was a big "people garden." She said that people are like flowers. They live together in the world like flowers grow in a garden. Red, yellow, small, tall—all growing together. They are all different. But each one is lovely.

Once a child said to Mrs. Bethune that blacks couldn't live in the "people garden." There were no black flowers! This made Mrs. Bethune feel sad. "Just because you have not seen a thing doesn't mean it doesn't exist," she always said.

Years later she got a wonderful surprise. While in the country of Holland, Mrs. Bethune was given the bulbs of black tulips—the first black flower. In Switzerland Mrs. Bethune was shown the black rose. This made her very happy.

Mrs. Bethune founded the National Council of Negro Women in 1935. She was a well-known speaker. She spoke at churches and schools all over the country.

"Just because you have not seen a thing doesn't mean it doesn't exist."

She ordered 72 black rose bushes. They were planted at Bethune-Cookman College. She also had black tulips planted at the entrance of her school.

Bert was the only child Mrs. Bethune had. He was a teacher too. On the wall at right is a picture of Mrs. Bethune's parents.

Mrs. Bethune was the first African-American woman to head a federal office. The NAACP awarded Mrs. Bethune the Spingarn Medal in 1935 for her work in the National Youth Administration. Standing beside her is Eleanor Roosevelt, Mrs. Bethune's good friend.

5

From Cotton Fields to the White House

In 1932 Franklin D. Roosevelt was elected President of the United States. The President asked Mrs. Bethune to serve in the **National Youth Administration (NYA).** She was the first African-American woman to hold a job that high up in the government. It was an honor.

Mrs. Eleanor Roosevelt was the president's wife. She was a friend to Mrs.

Bethune. At the time, some people didn't think a black person should be invited to the **White House**. But the Roosevelts did. Mrs. Bethune was always welcome at the White House and in the **Oval Office** too.

Once Mrs. Bethune went to see the President. " It is good to see you," he said.

Mrs. Bethune worked for many different causes. Here she is helping to raise money for cancer research.

"I don't know why," Mrs. Bethune answered. "I'm always asking for something."

"Yes," said the President, "but you never ask for yourself." It was true. Mrs. Bethune worked hard in the NYA. She tried to help young students find work so they could go to school. On April 25, 1945, Mrs. Bethune took part in the founding of the **United Nations**.

Groups would ask Mrs. Bethune to speak at special times like the graduation program above.

Mary protested for equal rights and fair treatment.

Countries from all over the world agreed to work together for peace.

Mrs. Bethune lived the rest of her life at Bethune-Cookman College. There she died of a **heart attack** on May 18, 1955.

The school that Mary McLeod Bethune started with $1.50 is still in Daytona Beach. It helps prove that hard work can make dreams come true.

Mrs. Bethune lived the last few years of her life at "The Retreat." It was her home on Bethune-Cookman College. She is also buried there. The marker says "Mother."

Words to Know

heart attack—An illness caused when a heart stops working properly. A person can die from a heart attack.

Moody Bible College—A college in Chicago started in 1886. It is now called the Moody Bible Institute.

National Youth Administration (NYA)—An organization that helps young people.

Oval Office—The President's office. It is oval-shaped.

president (PREZ-i-dent)—The leader of a country or group.

Scotia Seminary—An all-black school started in 1867 to teach former slaves and their children.

slave—A person who is owned by another. That person can be bought or sold.

United Nations—An organization of many countries who work together for peace.

White House—The house where the President of the United States lives.

Index